Becoming Yourself:

The Purpose of Man

Junior Anthony Baker

Becoming Yourself: The Purpose of a Man

Trilogy Christian Publishers

A Wholly Owned Subsidary of Trinity Broadcasting Network

2442 Michelle Drive

Tustin, CA 92780

For information, address Trilogy Christian Publishing

Rights Department, 2442 Michelle Drive, Tustin, Ca 92780.

Trilogy Christian Publishing/ TBN and colophon are trademarks of Trinity Broadcasting Network.

For information about special discounts for bulk purchases, please contact Trilogy Christian Publishing.

Manufactured in the United States of America

10 9 8 7 6 5 4 3 2 1

Library of Congress Cataloging-in-Publication Data is available.

ISBN 000-0-0000-0000-0

ISBN 000-0-0000-0000-0 (ebook)

Endorsements

It is not very often I read a book that catches me off guard; however, Inspire has done just that! Packed with wisdom paired with a practical approach, Junior's story will open your eyes to the fact that God planned for you. He created you with a purpose, and you are not here by accident. This book will transform you spiritually, emotionally, and physically from the inside out!

JT Jordan
Senior Pastor, Canvas Community Church

Junior Baker is not only a personal friend but also a powerful prayer partner. He and his wife, Racquel, work together as a ministry team. Seldom have I met a couple so committed to God. In this book, Junior shares how Christ called him out of darkness and into His marvelous light. His testimony speaks of God's might and power to overcome. Who knew that a young boy in Jamaica would be called to be a prayer warrior to America. I believe this is only the beginning of the volumes he will pen to glorify God. His commitment will challenge your Christian walk and draw you to ask how you can follow Christ more closely.

Patty Howell
Conference speaker and author of
Shoes in The Bible and Walking With God.

I first met Junior Baker in 2020 at Canvas Community Church in Manchester, Tennessee. After one Sunday morning service, Junior introduced himself and invited me to meet him for coffee so we could get acquainted. I'm not sure what prompted Junior to single me out, but I'm glad he did because it turned out to be a great meeting.

During our meeting, I discovered what a great man of God Junior was and how much he loved the Lord. We became great friends. Early in 2022, Junior announced he was writing a book and had gotten a commitment for publication. My book Entering Into God's Rest was published in 2001, so Junior asked me if I would be willing to edit his manuscript, and I agreed.

Junior's strengths are his love for the Holy Spirit and his earnest prayer life. His love and commitment to God come out clearly in every chapter of his book. Junior is one of the most devoted men of God that I have the pleasure of knowing.

Lowell Smith
Author of Entering Into God's Rest

TABLE OF CONTENTS

FOREWORD

I have known Junior Baker and his family for fifteen years. Our relationship started with him being my small group leader in a discipleship training school hosted by Youth With A Mission (YWAM). YWAM is an international, interdenominational, Christian organization whose motto is to know God and to make Him known.

Since knowing Mr. Baker, I have never seen him fall short in adopting YWAM's motto in his personal life. His passion for God and His word have not only allowed me to see his devotion in prayer and Bible study, but I have also been privileged to see him lead his household toward this same passion. I have seen Junior's children believe in God for funds for outreach and camps and watched God come through for them. My life has been challenged not only by Junior's passion but by the passion of his entire family.

In the pages of this inspiring book, you will not need to search hard to see the passion for Christ that Junior is pointing to you, the reader. As you read each page of this book, I hope you see the Holy Spirit at work and choose to partner with what the Holy Spirit wants to do in your heart.

After my discipleship training school with YWAM, I continued as a missionary with the organization for a decade, discipling scores of youths from across the nations and displaying the same level of faith, prayer, and love for God's word as I found in Junior, who is now my life friend. I am truly happy that God led us to cross paths more than a decade ago, and I am also happy you are holding this book in your hands. As Joy Dawson stated in her book Forever Ruined for the Ordinary, my prayers are that you, the reader, will be ruined for the ordinary faith and be called higher in your walk with the Lord.

Shawn Milton
CEO, S&S Life and Financial Services

INTRODUCTION

This book is an inspiring and motivational story of how my life was changed. It's also my testimony of the work of God and what the Holy Spirit did with my life. It opened my eyes to the wonders of who God is. I want to encourage and strengthen my readers who have been waiting for encouragement to go toward what they have been praying for. I discovered something amazing and unique about God early in my walk with Him. Since then, I've never allowed myself to think as I used to back in the days when I wanted to die. The truth behind this book is the transformation God took me through that I can put into a story and tell it like it is. I want my readers to know that it doesn't matter what they have gone through. They can still find hope and a future in a God that never stops loving us. I give credit only to God for all of the places I have been to, the people I have come in contact with, and what I have done. I continue to decrease so that He might continue to increase in me.

I hope this book will also help my readers understand the function of their true giftings and who they really are so they may become great. It is also an inspiration to anyone who wants to do more with his life and have that fire burning inside of them to go deeper into God. My prayer is that this book would take anyone who reads to a higher level in God. I believe that they will come face-to-face with the truth about what Jesus speaks of the Holy Spirit and be connected with the Holy Spirit. He is such an awesome person to know, love, teach and speak with. He turned my life completely around, and I've never been this happy in all my life before. I have never known such a thing existed, but I got a hold of what the word says in John 16:13–15. I had never been the same since I came in contact with the Holy Spirit.

Howbeit when he, the Spirit of truth, is come, he will guide you into all truth: for he shall not speak of himself; but whatsoever he shall hear, that shall he speak: and he will shew you things to come. He shall glorify me: for he shall receive of mine, and shall shew it unto you. All things that the Father hath are mine: therefore said I, that he shall take of mine, and shall shew it unto you.

John 16:13–15

We can walk in the prayers that Jesus prayed over us in John 17. It is, in my personal opinion, one of the greatest prayers ever prayed. These very powerful words have been directly spoken for us to walk in and I believe if we surpass our expectations as physical sons, we will walk into the true fulfillment as spiritual sons (John 1:12). My desire for this book is that many will have great encounters with the Holy Spirit and become children of God. That's what changes everything about who we are, our purpose, our calling, and our gifting to become all that we are created to become.

We Were Planned

God has a place in every person created by Him. He has purposes, visions, and goals. What are God's purposes, visions, and goals for our lives? How does that look? What do they mean? What is God's heart toward us? Every person has to answer these questions for themselves. Let me answer in this way. We all have to give an account because we were planned for: we did not just happen by chance.

What we are and what we are to become is already fulfilled and completed in God. That, my friend, is to come into His presence, know Him, and walk in all He has planned for us. I am going to share a little about myself and His plans over my life because His plans prevail (Isaiah 46:10–11).

I'll mark all of this down throughout this book. Let me start this way. I didn't learn to read until I was in my twenties, and now, fifteen years later, I am writing this book. It is one of many which are to come. I am writing with my own hands, by myself. How could this happen and become possible? You see, I started to understand my purpose in God and that God has already accomplished it. It's already completed in Him; it is marked down. Everything from God that is for me was placed in me. All that I am to become and walk in. As we walk, we discover; as we discover, we see; as we see, we do; as we do, we become; as we become, we are fulfilled. That is what we are designed for. I'll share more about myself as I go on in this book, for writing this is just a small testimony of what God has called me to do.

Understand This

Understand this when we come in contact with God, Himself. It is mind-blowing, my friends! We, therefore, become transformed and changed by getting a glimpse into what God has for us. We become like Paul in Philippians 3:13, "Brethren, I count not myself to have apprehended: but this one thing I do, forgetting those things which are behind, and reaching forth unto those things which are before."

We must leave everything behind us and press toward the things ahead, toward our purpose. The things that are meaningless become meaningful. The key to all of this is to pursue, know, and understand God's purpose for our lives and its value. For example, what is the purpose of a seed? A lot of people would say it is to become a tree, but I am saying to all who think that way, no. Why? You may ask. Because a seed is a tree, right? But is being a tree its one and only purpose? Is that all God created it for? Just to be a tree? Again, I say no. Let me ask you a question: is your only purpose just to exist? Is that the only intent of God, the Maker's, heart and purpose for you or me?

What God creates: us, the world, the universe, and everything is beautiful and mind-blowing, my friends! The purpose of a tree is seen in many man-made things: beautiful art sculptures, pieces of furniture made out of wood in your living room, and even in some of the most expensive cars designed into the dashboard or fender in a unique way. If we only see a seed as a tree, we will never see the purpose, value, or potential of what God designed for it to become. You and I are way more advanced. Start seeing yourself the way you truly are, and become what you are created and designed to be.

We are masterpieces designed and created beautifully to be perfected by God. We understand the purpose of the trees starting from seed, yet that is nothing compared to the greatness in us and what we are created for. We are the ones God allows to design and shape the trees into their true potentials and purposes when we make all of these beauties from them. These abilities were placed in us uniquely by God, and that in itself is amazing! When I understood how powerful and unique I am (man is) it not only blew my mind, but also transformed everything about me. I became unstoppable! I started asking God a lot of questions, questions like, what is my purpose? What are your visions and plans for my life? I started spending hours, days, weeks, months, and years praying, fasting, and asking Him about me.

I remember fasting for seven days, absolute fasting! I only had water four days out of the seven, and boy did He speak as if He literally walked in the room! I thought I was going to die! I said, "God, stop. Don't talk to me anymore." I cannot explain or express the way it happened. God never stopped. He started revealing everything to me by nations and continents. I could not contain what had been revealed to me! I remember crying for about two to three hours coming from Mexico. He showed me a glimpse of my purpose and what I exist for.

The next morning I woke up crying and telling God that I just wanted to do what He wanted me to do. My eyes were opened, and I started to cry because I woke up seeing and believing, knowing who I am and what I must do because God showed me my purpose. Dr. Myles Munroe said, "The graveyard is the richest place on the surface of earth." Millions, or may I say, billions, have died not knowing they were created for a purpose. They died not fully doing or giving what they should have done or given to this world! The key question here is, family, do you want that to happen to you? Many of us are faithful and committed to our jobs and churches, which is good. I am for that because I am committed too. But have we ever stopped to think about who we really are? We are treasures hidden in earthen vessels.

*For God, who commanded the light to shine out of darkness, hath
shined in our hearts, to give the light of the knowledge of the glory of
God in the face of Jesus Christ. But we have this treasure in earthen
vessels, that the excellency of the power may be of God, and not of us.*

2 Corinthians 4:6–7

Have you ever asked yourself what this beautiful treasure is?
Are you seeing yourself the way God sees you? Do you know what
you are and that you can become all that you are born to be? Let
me encourage you to change your life pattern, change your thought
process, and get outside the box. Become you, the one who is created
in God's image and His likeness. The masterpiece in you does not fit
in the world but in Him because we are in God and in Christ. Jesus,
my friends, does not fit in the world, but He will change everything
in you if you give Him the chance to do so.

When we become who we truly are, we fulfill God's purpose in
us. We agree with the visions and purposes God has for our life, and
say yes to it all. We now see the big beyond and above without limits.
We should now be able to understand we were not just born to live
a natural life. See it this way, if we are created in His Image and His
likeness, then who are we like? Answer that question for yourself. He
is unique and different and not to be compared to anything or anyone,
not even you or me. I want you to understand what I am saying. He
made us with some of His attributes. He creates and makes us creative
as well. So we should then change the way we think. Our mentality
must take on a different approach. When I see and understand who
I am in God, I say, My Lord! You would never know how much I am
transformed. This transformation caused this book to be written. I
became unstoppable, quit my job, and started my business with little
money at all. You see, I have found my true purpose in life! What is

yours? What are you passionate about? What is the thing that, when you think about it, gives you fulfillment? Don't let it go to sleep. Your true purpose is to live. That is the very reason your purpose was created by God for and in you. I cannot tell you what that is in you. You have to know what it is. If you don't know, ask God, your Maker. He will show you what it is; believe me, He will! I am not kidding you. That is what changed my life! I ask Him, and He answers me. Listen to this verse:

> *For I know the thoughts that I think toward you, saith the LORD, thoughts of peace, and not of evil, to give you an expected end. Then shall ye call upon me, and ye shall go and pray unto me, and I will hearken unto you. And ye shall seek me, and find me, when ye shall search for me with all your heart.*

Jeremiah 29:11–13

We are that masterpiece in Him. The beauty about this is that He knows who we are and what we have the ability to do. He wants us to become that: to be fulfilled and to leave this earth knowing not that we are perfect but that we have pleased our Maker and knowing we have changed and made a difference in this world. Dr. Martin Luther King Jr. has done it. Nelson Mandela, Abraham Lincoln, Mother Teresa, John Wesley, Martin Luther, and many more have done it, and I can go on and on. We cannot afford to live our lives without purpose or meaning. We are way more precious than that. We are too valuable and strategically designed not to become who we truly are. It does not matter where we are now to come into our God-given purpose.

God's Effect on Us

God's kingdom comes on earth in its fullness, not just to sit on earth. His kingdom comes, and He is continually being revealed through His son Jesus Christ. It has been seen and manifests in us today. It causes those that come into His presence to be changed, challenged, and chase after something that is beyond us. I remember there was a movement of God in church one Sunday night. I believe I was about one and a half years as a believer. I was very young and did not understand much at the time, but I was always wanting more from God, so I couldn't wait to get home to talk to Him! I got home, and for about four to five hours, I was there crying and talking to God, asking Him about me, and worshipping Him. I got tired, so I tried to sleep. I turned off the lights and got in bed. As I closed my eyes, the presence of God came into the room. There was a bright light, so I opened my eyes because I thought my brother had turned the light on. But the room was dark, so I closed my eyes. The light was there. I could do nothing but cry before Him. That night was so powerful and special I did not want it to end.

Our identity is in Him. He is the one we should be passionate about. In Him, we have hope; in Him, we are secure. Our fulfillment should not be in anyone or anything but Him. Does this mean we cannot do anything else? God would love for us to have fulfillment in life. God wants us to know fulfillment first comes from Him, and He takes priority. See, I found fulfillment that night when His presence came into my room in that bright light and filled me up. That is the most beautiful feeling ever. I love my wife and children like crazy, but as much as I love them, God comes first because I love Him more.

This is my commandment, that ye love one another, as I have loved you. Greater love hath no man than this, that a man lay down his life for his friends. Ye are my friends, if ye do whatsoever I command you. Henceforth I call you not servants; for the servant knoweth not what his lord doeth: but I have called you friends; for all things that I have heard of my Father I have made known unto you. Ye have not chosen me, but I have chosen you, and ordained you, that ye should go and bring forth fruit, and that your fruit should remain: that whatsoever ye shall ask of the Father in my name, he may give it to you.

John 15:12–16

Only when a person finds himself in God and the truth is revealed, can such a man see that which is pleasing to Him. To understand what it is to live in Him is not something simple. It is big. It is what makes us different. It is what changes the system around us, our mindset and mentality, and approach. It propels us into understanding the keys to lock and unlock heaven. When we come in contact with God's plans for us, everything changes. We explode to a different level. We are ripped apart inside and out. This has been a challenge for me as I am writing. I pray you will never be the same again as you are reading this book. Read Genesis 1–3. Read it in depth. I believe it is the foundation by which God makes Himself known. His existence to mankind goes even deeper because He became more intimate with us when He formed us. Even though He thought of us, He blessed us when He breathed into us His Spirit the breath of life. He never stopped loving us. He shared a deep relationship with Adam by walking and talking with him every day. My friend, I believe He wants to share that very same intimacy with us today. How beautiful and amazing it is when we find ourselves in His presence.

God and Us

What God shared with us is amazing. When He said to Adam to be fruitful and multiply and have dominion over the earth, He was saying to all of us within Adam: to become all He has created us to be. The world was only water, animals, and trees, and from there, God allowed mankind to shape the world into what it is today. We now have continents, nations, and cities. God gave us this world, yes He did, and we bring it to what it is today. Where is your part that God has given you to continue shaping His creation? Before a man becomes himself, he must first understand the power and dominion given to him by God.

> *So God created man in his own image, in the image of God created he him; male and female created he them. And God blessed them, and God said unto them, be fruitful, and multiply, and replenish the earth, and subdue it: and have dominion over the fish of the sea, and over the fowl of the air, and over every living thing that moveth upon the earth.*

Genesis 1:27–28

What does it mean to become yourself? It simply means knowing and understanding the God's will, plans, and purposes over our lives, so that we can fully operate and function in what He wants us to do. This book is not about big, fancy words. It is about coming face-to-face with God, Himself, and for us to know Him more because when we fully function in God's will over our lives, we bring the known into the unknown and reflect God on earth.

Becoming yourself is a true reflection of who God is because we represent Him throughout creation here on earth. We are molded in His image and likeness. We are children of God. "For we are His workmanship, created in Christ Jesus unto good works, which God hath before ordained that we should walk in them" (Ephesians 2:10).

His creation, His reflection, His love, His beauty, and His delight are in us. We must never forget who we are and whose we are and who we reflect. Because these three words mean so much and are so powerful when we actually know and understand what they mean. Let's take a closer look at them.

The Greek word ASAH means "to create," "to build," "to accomplish," and "to fulfill." TSELEM means "Resemblance" and a "representative figure." DMUWTH, likeness, simply means "a pattern."

What is His heart toward us? Why did He make us this way, with so many attributes of Himself? He is a triune God: Father, Son, and Holy Spirit. We are body, soul, and spirit. He creates, and we also create. He gives us this earth, and He wants us to take charge. If we get this in the core of our spirit and see ourselves the way God designed us, we are unstoppable.

According to my earnest expectation and my hope, that in nothing I shall be ashamed, but that with all boldness, as always, so now also Christ shall be magnified in my body, whether it be by life, or by death. For to me to live is Christ, and to die is gain.

Philippians 1:20–21

My, my, my, that is why I am not afraid to die. The Holy Spirit taught me how to read and write! You see, I could not read at age twenty, and now I am writing a book, and there is no book I cannot read. I've read so many books since I became transformed. Not that I compare myself to God or want us to compare ourselves with God, but the way we are designed is so we can become so much more! I believe the Father would be proud of us. Every level we choose to go, He wants us to go there, and He wants us to become all He has created us to become. I was born into a very poor family and grew up in poverty. Now, I own my own business, I have gone on missions, and I have traveled to many nations, sometimes leading a team, sometimes being led by teams. I have traveled first class, shared stages with Grammy award winners, and been interviewed by one of the biggest Jamaican religious television shows viewed by millions. I have been on TV at different times and even been with and shaken hands with the prime ministers of different countries.

I will stop at nothing. I will not stop myself. God will not stop me either. He doesn't want me to fail, nor does He want you to fail. He wants us to walk in the greatest manifestation of His presence ever. How great that is, is up to us and how aggressively we've stepped into His presence. God is the light of the world, and we are justified by Him: not by society, not by culture, but by Him. We take this light and shine it into the cities and dark places and bring change. There is nothing like us that exists. We are special and unique and that is why we will never be loved by the enemy, Satan. He will always hit us and try to stop us from walking in purpose and fulfillment. That's why he is so jealous of us and does not like us at all.

His Presence with Us

Come with me on this journey because the power and purpose of a man are given to him by God. Greatness is not for one's own pleasure but found in God. The journey of a man does not begin with the man, but long ago with God Himself before creation was and before man was formed in his mother's womb. His plans and purposes were established in us all.

Remember the former things of old: for I am God, and there is none else; I am God, and there is none like me, declaring the end from the beginning, and from ancient times the things that are not yet done, saying, my counsel shall stand, and I will do all my pleasure:

Isaiah 46:9–10

A man's potential is in God, his Maker. Therefore it is not what he does but what God does in and through him if he lets Him. It is God who leads, directs, and guides, so now you can only find your true sense of purpose when you know how valuable you are in God's hand. As you read this book, let me ask you a question: Do you know who you are and why you exist? Because for a man to be dominant, he must first answer this question, "Who am I? Do you know?" If the answer is yes, he knows, and I believe that as a believer goes on, he will be strengthened. If your answer is no to this question, if you do not know who you are, your life could be radically transformed and challenged by the end of this book. I believe that His presence with us is so effective because God has strategically designed every one of us placed on earth to be His ambassadors.

We are Powerful

Our existence is more powerful than we could ever think or imagine! I love it! We exist to be fulfilled, which means that inside of us is the greatness and the ability to do above and beyond. Remember, we are made in His image and likeness, and He breathes into us a part of Himself which gives us life. We become living beings and whatever comes from us is a part of God who gives us that life. We are a part of Him. That is so beautiful! A part of Him is in our DNA. To reflect Him and to know that if all of this greatness of God is in us is to

23

know that we are more than ordinary people. We should be the ones that shape churches, schools, workplaces, communities, families, and homes. We have answers to questions and we give solutions. With Christ in us, we are the driving force. We make the world and people better. We are all completed in God. Are you going to let His purpose be complete on earth for you, as it is in heaven? God completes us, sees and knows what we are, and then tells us to become all that we can because He knows the end from the beginning. He said this boldly.

So, who are we like? Are we like our Maker, God? Then we, therefore must reflect Him in our everyday life. We are a resemblance of Him here on earth. That means we must function the way He wants us to; His will be done on earth as in heaven. We bring the supernatural into the natural, the seen into the unseen. When we walk into our purpose and identity in God, He works miracles, signs, and wonders through us.

It is for our God-given purpose that we live. It is what drives us to become who we truly are. It is within us to do beyond and above. We are like the one that covers himself "with the light as with a garment" (Psalms 104:1–2). That light shines in and through us. We are never ourselves but always His, never alone but carrying His presence everywhere we go, reflecting the true beauty of God, our Maker.

WE ARE CHILDREN

Children: that is who we are. Molded, designed, and fashioned in God, our Father's image, we carry in us the DNA of our Father, which makes us uniue in creation. Therefore if we are committed to being before Him, in His presence, we will reflect Him the way Jesus reflects Him among us on earth. As children, our will, purpose, and calling should always reflect our Father.

When we walk in the understanding of our potential as a child of God, it is key to walk out our purpose. In walking out our purpose, we are also walking in the ability to fulfill our Father's will. A good relationship includes the most beautiful times we could ever have with our Father. By spending time with the Father as true children, we will understand the heart of the Father for our life.

Jesus walked in power and authority with signs and wonders. Why? Because He walked in fulfillment of His Father.

Then answered Jesus and said unto them, Verily, verily, I say unto you, the Son can do nothing of himself, but what he seeth the Father do: for what things soever he doeth, these also doeth the   Son likewise. For the Father loveth the Son, and sheweth him all things that himself doeth: and he will shew him greater works than these, that ye may marvel.

John 5:19–20

Jesus says the very same words to us,

Verily, verily, I say unto you, He that believeth on me, the works that I do shall he do also; and   greater works than these shall he do; because I go unto my Father. And whatsoever ye shall ask in my name, that will I do, that the Father may be glorified in the Son.

John 14:12–13

In this beautiful and amazing way, Jesus describes our purpose as sons accomplished in our Father's work and speaks this into our lives here on earth. If we are going to walk in power and authority, we must pattern our life after the life of Jesus. This is one of the most beautiful examples I could ever share of a son expressing the love, unity, commitment, oneness, and obedience of walking in fulfillment of his Father and doing it well, as it is assigned.

We have to master the way that Jesus serves His Father. The Father takes great joy and pleasure in watching us become who we truly are, what He created us to become. This is so powerful! You see, my brothers and sisters, this is why nothing can stand before Jesus. I mean nothing, no man, no demons, nothing on earth or that is to come. The way He honors His Father is amazing, and this is why His Father honors Him with authority on earth.

The Purpose of a Son

It is through knowing we are sons and daughters that we can run with joy and fulfillment in who we truly are! Have you ever been in a place of dissatisfaction or failure and wanted to give up on life? That was me. At one point, I was nothing in life, just smoking and on the street every day. I could not read or put a sentence together, saying to God, "I want to die," and thinking, just take my life. Years later, I am writing a book and ministering with some of the greatest leaders! God, your Father, will never give up on you, so don't you dare give up on yourself. The Father did not give up on the prodigal son. He accepts us as His children, and that will never change. We accept Him when we walk as sons, as the scripture says:

But as many as received him, to them gave he power to become the sons of God, even to them that believe on His name: which were born, not of blood, nor of the will of the flesh, nor of the will of man, but of God.

John 1:12–13

It is an honor to serve when we accept who God made us! The key to understanding and connecting with God is to stay in His Word, which makes a difference in us. His word is what sets us on fire as children of the living God.

What changed my life is the Word of the living God. I picked up the Bible and started reading it. I did not understand it at the time because I could not read. However, I would read the Bible every day. The more I read, the more God taught me. I started to understand the Word. Looking back, it brings tears to my eyes. The things that God has taught! The Holy Spirit has been my main teacher and inspiration. My focus has been the Holy Spirit. I developed a spiritual relationship with Him that changed my life forever. It is unbelievable. He has brought me from nowhere and placed me where I am today. I am proud to be a son of the most-high God! This has pushed me into my purpose and helped me to walk the way I walk in honor of my Father today, fearing nothing and no man, but instead being as bold as I can be. That is the posture and position I have taken on the earth, walking in honor of the Father the way Jesus did. I will never stop!

The moment I came in contact with the presence of the Holy Spirit and He started to teach me, and I began to gain knowledge of how to read, and started to read and write. My life started to become something different. In those moments and times, I began to understand the purpose of being a son of the most-high God. I treasure that sonship with the Father every day because it makes me better and better. I am a different person. We can all become sons and daughters of the most-high God on this earth we walk on today. Become yourself and find your true potential. That is how God created you. The mark of Christ is on us. Let us tear apart the box. Let us walk in fulfillment of our true ability that the Father has strategically created in us and purposely placed in us on earth for we "can do all things through Christ which strengtheneth me" (Philippians 4:13).

Nay, in all these things we are more than conquerors through him that loved us. For I am persuaded that neither death, nor life, nor angels, nor principalities, nor powers, nor things present, nor things to come, nor height, nor depth, nor any other creature, shall be able to separate us from the love of God, which is in Christ Jesus our LORD.

Romans 8:37–39

I remember spending so much time with the Holy Spirit. My focus then is still my focus now. I was so committed to being in His presence. I would come home from work, get showered, put cologne on, dress nicely, pray and worship Him. I would do it every day and never wanted it to end. I fell in love with Him so much that I didn't want to leave His presence. It was as if I was hugged, kissed, loved, and embraced by my Father every day, and I did not want to lose that as a son. His presence meant everything to me then, and it means everything to me today. As I write this book today, I am still passionate about my heavenly Father, the same way I was those years ago.

There is nothing else like the presence of the living God. Nothing is more beautiful to the Father than to have His children come and love on Him. He loves it. I meet with Him every day at a set time. I remember one day coming from work, I stopped and talked with a friend. The conversation went on longer than it should have, and boy,

I tell you, God did not like that at all. For the first time in my life, I felt His hand touch me. What was so different about the touch? It wasn't just a touch; He was pulling my shirt so hard and so strong I told my friend, "I have to go." I am telling you the truth about the relationship we have. I could not wait to get home because I knew and understood the touch of my Father. I met with Him that night, and it was magical. Since that day, if I am talking with someone when I should be meeting with Him at a specific time, He pulls my shirt and I love it. Being in His presence is always magical. I love His presence more and more every day. It's the most beautiful, peaceful, precious, and honorable place to be to this day. I have never felt anything like it on earth and have never felt anything like it in my body. He has taken me to a different realm. I pray over you as you read that his presence will take you to a different place in Him.

The purpose of His children is to be in the Father's presence, to know the rhythm of His heartbeat, to know His instructions and understand them, and to walk in full obedience to them. I love when my own children obey me and follow my instructions. It is then easier for me to point them to God, their true Father. To become that child to Him is what the Lord requires from us. When we walk in this manner, we walk in full authority and dominion on the earth as children of the most-high God. "But as many as received him, to them gave he power to become the sons of God, even to them that believe on his name" (John 1:12).

There's no a hunger for His presence in the world today as in times past. People hunger for the things of the world. Let's not lose His presence; don't lose His passion.

Yet I have left me seven thousand in Israel, all the knees which have not bowed to Baal, and every mouth which hath not kissed him. So he departed thence, and found Elisha the son of Shaphat, who was plowing with twelve yoke of oxen before him, and he with the twelfth: and Elijah passed by him, and cast his mantle upon him.

1 Kings 19:18–19

I believe that few walk in true sonship with the Father who and have not bowed their knees to the systems of this world. God still has faithful sons and daughters running after Him today. Let us be a part of this remnant, running after Him on the earth today.

I am delighted to be called a son every day! I want to love and hug and kiss Him and be with Him, and what is so amazing is that the more I love the Father, the more I want to do His will. The more I want to do His will, the more I love Him. The more I love Him, the more passionate I am about His will for my life. There is a love I have found for Him that I cannot explain. Whatever He tells me to do, I do it, which is the most honorable thing for me. My purpose is to serve God in this life in the world I am in today.

What makes you passionate? What gives you motivation? What makes you feel like you can take on the world? For me, the most beautiful and amazing answer to these questions is the relationship of a son's heart to his father and the response from a father's heart to his son. When we connect with the Father, we know and become passionate about the direction of our life. When we feel His heartbeat, there is no greater motivation. That, my beloved brothers and sisters, makes us run without fear to take on the world, walking in such passion to the things of God. That's when we feel like and know that we can take on the world in the way that God wants us to, the way that brings Him glory, causing an impact in the world around us that society cannot change. The worldly systems cannot change us because our connection with the Father influences the world and all that is happening around us when we connect with the Father. Jesus said, "I and the Father are one" (John 10:30, NIV) and that he speaks "the things which I have seen with my Father: and ye also do the things which ye heard from your father" (John 8:38, ASV).

This is the connection I'm talking about when I talk about becoming one with the Father, understanding what He's saying so we release what he hear Him say when we speak. We lay hands on the sick and change their circumstances and situation because we do what we see the Father do. What is the intent of the Father for us, and what does that look like? Let me say it in a simple form:

Jesus therefore answered and said unto them, Verily, verily, I say unto you, The Son can do nothing of himself, but what he seeth the Father doing: for what things soever he doeth, these the Son also doeth in like manner.

John 5:19 (ASV)

If we are going to walk in full power and authority, this is the example we should pattern ourselves after. Nothing like it has ever been seen on earth. The relationship Jesus has with the Father is our example of how we should walk with Him on earth, walking in His presence to do what He wants us to do. In the same way, this is the relationship God our Father wants to have with us. He wants us to know what He is saying, the way Jesus said, I do what I see my Father do, I speak what I hear Him speak. God wants us to feel his heartbeat, to walk in dominion, and release what He is saying to us on the earth today,

Know that the Father will never hide anything from us. He will share everything He's doing on the earth with us as He did with Abraham, "And Jehovah said, Shall I hide from Abraham that which I do" (Genesis 18:17, ASV).

God is waiting for us to walk in true sonship unto Him on earth today, but why? Because he wants us to walk in our true purpose and potential. I believe this closeness with the Father brings us to the true meaning of why He created us, the reason for our existence. That's where the true meaning and fulfillment come from, and that is why Jesus is our biggest example and should be our main focus in walking with the Father.

We can shape our spiritual walk with God in so many areas. There are so many ways we can get help in developing and understanding our gifts to fulfill what God has called us to. One such help to me is Youth With a Mission (YWAM). I spent nine years in YWAM learning the foundation of missions. YWAM has shaped my walk into a leader. YWAM became a great coach for what God wanted to do in my life today. I recommend anyone who wants to know and develop more about their calling with God to seek out YWAM, especially if there is a call on your life to go to the nations of the earth. YWAM is the place to start. They are all over the world. I recommend that you look them up. They have contributed to the man I have become today and the love and passion I have for my mission to go to the nations of the earth.

One of the hardest things to find today is a spiritual father who mentors, leaders, and guides us, with accountability, as believers to grow and shape our walk with God. In my early walk with God, my spiritual father, Major Neil Lewis, introduced me to YWAM and sent my family and me there. He played a key role in my early walk with the Lord. God had been the center of my life, but I needed a spiritual father and mentorship as I grew in my early walk with God. God is my first father, maker, and master designer, and I love Him more than anything or anyone in this world, and I will never compare Him to anyone or anything in this world.

Having a spiritual father gives us guidance, mentorship, and accountability. Understanding the potential of a child of God is the key to walking in our full purpose and calling. Submission and authority to leadership are the keys as sons, especially as new believers, to our hunger and passion for God and to zealously go after the things of God. We need these men and women in our lives to guide us to where God wants to take and place us in life. It is easier to walk in obedience with God our Father when we walk in sonship every day with these mentors. We are molded and shaped to fulfill the Father's will in our lives, but we must be true to ourselves and submit to our earthly leadership and guides. We will become powerful and walk into dominion as Jesus did on earth when we obey those who are set above us, walking as God wants us to. We can fulfill His will in our lives as Jesus did. God is amazing!

This is also a heartbreaker for me. We will slowly lose our generation day by day if we continue walking outside of sonship with God our Father. I believe as leaders in the body of Christ today and as spiritual fathers, we have to see those potentials in our presence. We must become the engine or conduit to get them going, mentoring young men and women of God. I believe sons are crying out for fathers today, but so many have been misled and guide our generation today away from the Father. I don't want to be misunderstood when I say "sons" I am speaking of sons and daughters within the body of Christ and even those who have not yet become Christians and followers of Jesus Christ. There are many gifts among them that can contribute to God's work today. I want you to see it clearly through the heart of John 1:12 (ASV), "But as many as received him, to them gave he power to become the sons of God, even to them that believe on his name." And that is exactly what we are, children: we are His.

This is what I am saying, once we know who we are in God and that we are handmade and fashioned by Him, we will surrender everything to Him and walk in His will. One of the most beautiful examples to follow is of Abraham and his son Isaac. Abraham had a son and surrendered him to God his Father in the most remarkable way! Abraham responded obediently when God told him to sacrifice his son, Isaac. This is where we all need to be as children of the most-high God today. God could have just said, "now I know Abraham that you fear me." He also asked for Abraham's willingness to offer Isaac. Isaac's response to his father, Abraham, was unbelievable, as seen in Genesis 22:1–19. It's the same way Jesus responded to God his Father in Luke 22:42–44.

Picture this: these faithful children all walked in the fulfillment of their purpose, calling, and assignment. This is why they existed and accomplished what God wanted them to accomplish. Their lives were purposeful and meaningful on earth. We all need to be like this.

In His Mind

Becoming yourself and walking in your purpose and potential is not something God is trying to figure out for your life, nor is it something you need to reserve for when you become an adult. From the beginning, you and I were destined to become great. "Before I formed thee in the belly I knew thee; and before thou camest forth out of the womb I sanctified thee, and I ordained thee a prophet unto the nations" (Jeremiah 1:5).

God might not say it to you as he said to Jeremiah, you are a "prophet to the nations" (Jeremiah 1:5, NIV), but I want you to know and understand as you read that you are a complete package. He knew your greatness before He formed you in your mother's womb and has made you all that you are.

Please don't ever forget this: you are worth so much; you are valuable to God; you are a masterpiece. As you are reading, I want you to pull apart from the limitations and expectations of man, find yourself in the complete purposes of God's will over your life, and come into the greatness that He has placed you on earth to claim. Become that which God designed you to be. What does that look like for you? That's something you have to answer for yourself by being in His presence and allowing Him to unfold His mind, His heart desires, and His intentions over your life. I don't know what that looks like for you, but I know what He said about me. That is why I'm writing this book. I could not read, and I could not write. I did not understand a thing. I was blank, but He told me who I am, I began to read as He taught me how. Then I read what He says about me in Jeremiah, and I understood that I could become all God created me to be. I find a sense of purpose and value concerning who I am in God. You must know where your place of influence is on this earth and live to your full potential because I believe we all carry that masterpiece from that master designer and builder within us.

For I know the thoughts that I think toward you, saith the LORD, thoughts of peace, and not of evil, to give you an expected end. Then shall ye call upon me, and ye shall go and pray unto me, and I will hearken unto you. And ye shall seek me, and find me, when ye shall search for me with all your heart. And I will be found of you, saith the LORD: and I will turn away your captivity, and I will gather you from all the nations, and from all the places whither I have driven you, saith the LORD; and I will bring you again into the place whence I caused you to be carried away captive.

Jeremiah 29:11–14

God clearly expresses His thoughts for us. In other words, He wants us to know that we are always in His mind. In the above verse, He tells us of His plans for our lives and how they are to prosper us. He tells us it's already done. His thoughts are consumed with our greatest gifts, talents, dreams, and potential. He wants us to tap into it and fulfill them all. His thoughts are always filled with expectations for a relationship with us. His greatest desire is that we would walk with Him again just as Adam did before.

He wants us to know in every moment that in Him we find all that life has to offer, as a father has a friend and a healer has a savior. He wants to share all of Himself with us. We are a reflection of Him, and He wants us to reflect Him because He knows the power within us. That is why He said in Jeremiah 29:13 (NCV), "when you search for me with all your heart you will find me" He wants to display Himself through us in full.

If you are feeling a greater hunger to be deeper in Him, please do not hold anything back from God, because He will not hold anything back from us. Believe that He wants us to go in-depth about what He has for us. When Jesus said "greater works than these" (John 14:12) we shall do, He meant every single word. My question is, do we believe what He said? Do we understand what He means?

I will now share about the Holy Spirit, the amazing third person of the trinity, His role, and how He empowered the twelve disciples. We have all read what they did in the New Testament and how they transformed the world with the empowering and fulfilling presence of the Holy Spirit. I believe it's the same thing God wants for us in today's world: to empower us with the Holy Spirit to fulfill His desires for us.

When we come into close contact with the Holy Spirit, we will know God's greater thoughts about us. His mind is revealed to us because we are in that closeness with God, and with the leading of the Holy Spirit, we can move in perfect rhythm and sequence with the movement of God. I will talk more about the Holy Spirit and go deeper in another chapter because He is the one that changed my life. He's the one who empowered me. I was at home one night, just coming from church, and needed so much more from God. There was a move of the presence of God at church, and I came home with that hunger. For four hours, I worshipped the Lord. The Holy Spirit came into my room that night! It was the brightest light I have ever seen in my life. He hit me with His presence; I have never been the same. The Holy Spirit is who transforms us and brings us into the nature of who we are in the relationship with God our Father to emulate the role of Jesus Christ, the son. When we capture these, we walk in the authority and power of who we are and do great things for the kingdom of God!

Question: Have you ever asked God why He created you? Or what is the intention, thoughts, or reason for you? These are questions that will change your life forever as these questions bring you close to God. When we reason with Him, talk with Him, and ask Him questions about us, He responds, and His greatness comes to life!

Come now, and let us reason together, saith the LORD: though your sins be as scarlet, they shall be as white as snow; though they be red like crimson, they shall be as wool. If ye be willing and obedient, ye shall eat the good of the land:

Isaiah 1:18–19

From the beginning, we were always in God's heart and mind. The truth is, we would be blown away by how God thinks about us: The truth about His heart as a father toward us and the relationship with us. He has no intentions of hiding anything from us. We are the ones hiding from Him. We are the ones who don't want to know who we are in Him. We are the ones who are not asking the questions about the power that has been invested, given, and is living in us, and we are the ones holding back what He wants to reveal. He wants to reason with us; He wants us to ask Him the questions, but do we want to know God's plans for us to become all He created us to become? Or are we afraid of the challenges, how our lives will be reshaped, or the path we must take for Him? Are we afraid of becoming greater than the world's expectations or what society and systems say about us? That we can't amount to anything? Are we going to allow the world to determine our greatness? Are we going to allow the system of this world to put limits on what we can do? Or are we going to accept our ability to become great in God? We can only stop ourselves from becoming what God has destined us to become and walking in fulfillment by not going after the heart of God and seeking His presence and relationship. Our testimony will be to change the systems of this world and bring the kingdom of God here on earth, so it becomes visible. The kingdom Jesus talks about is the kingdom of God within us, and it will reflect all God says we are.

He is calling us to a greater relationship with Him; that is His goal. My question is, how much will we have and know of Him if we do not have a connection with Him? A relationship is the most important thing to God when it comes to us. I believe that is the position from which God directs us. To come into greater glory with God is to clear our minds and hearts, allow our spirits to be free, and cleanse ourselves from the systems of this world so that we can completely focus our minds and hearts on the things of God. "Let this mind be in you, which was also in Christ Jesus"(Philippians 2:5).

If we want to reflect the presence of the Holy Spirit, there must be a movement in us. Loving the world or the things of the world is not an option. We can't be attached to the world. We can live in the world, but we become the changers and the character God wants us to display in the world so that He is glorified. John said it in this way:

Love not the world, neither the things that are in the world. If any man love the world, the love of the Father is not in him. For all that is in the world, the lust of the flesh, and the lust of the eyes, and the pride of life, is not of the Father, but is of the world.

1 John 2:15-16

I truly believe that we can be in the world and not of it, and that's hen we will walk in full dominion and power in the earth: when it has nothing on us. For us to come into greater glory with God, we have to destroy the things of the world and come into alignment with

God's plans for us. I am not saying we can't take part in the world. Yes, we can take part in it and dominate it. We can dominate in sports, our workplace, our schools, our businesses, etc., but what I am saying is, don't let these things take you away from God's purposes and plans. While you are in these areas, in these places of influence, sports, business, schools, and entertainment, don't let these take you away from God's plan. Instead, let the light of Christ shine in you and bring glory to Him in all you do.

Clear the things of this world from your minds and hearts so that you will not be attached to them, and tap into the mind of Christ Jesus. Commune with the Holy Spirit, the presence of the living God that leads us into our purpose and gives us directions regarding our calling with God. All of this is so we can understand the ways of God for our lives and walk in them, or may I say manifest in them the movements and rhythm of how God wants us to flow within the earth so that He can be the true reflection in us and the scripture will be fulfilled. "Your kingdom come, Your will be done on earth as it is in heaven" (Matthew 6:10, NIV).

I know I have asked many questions in these few chapters, and I will ask more as I write. These questions will change our lives forever if we ask them and allow them to be answered. Questions like, why did Jesus die? There has to be a reason for that. Thinking about that in the right context will blow our minds! Why did he redeem us back to the Father? These are powerful questions because these questions are what take us to the next level in knowing God, our Father. The Father wants us to experience Him in all that we can, and He wants us to live these experiences to the fullest on earth. Everything I say is about reflecting Him so that He can bring greater glory to the earth.

Our Thought Process

Our greatest movement is our thought process. Can you imagine that? The way we process the things we pursue is amazing! Most of the time, we do this with such urgency and aggressiveness! We make every effort to get our plans done or accomplished. What if we approach God with that same mentality? Let us know his intentions for our life and be in harmony with God our Father and His plans for us. Understanding that our minds and the way we process things go only as far as we will allow them to go, the nature of who we are in God is amazing! We have the choice to unlock the beautiful mind of God! This will allow us to walk in full agreement and obedience to our Father and how He thinks about us. Wow! It is mind-blowing to walk in a relationship with understanding! I process what He is reveals to me and walk in a great relationship with my Father because my mind and thoughts are on Him. This makes us different as sons and daughters, as children of God. This is what separates us, makes His light shine through us, and what makes God proud of us. If we honor Him, I believe when the end of our time on earth comes we will hear "Well done thou good and faithful servant enter into my kingdom that I have prepared for you" (Matthew 25:21).

This book is different. It does not give you all the details, walk you step-by-step through "one way to pursue God", or give you all the answers you might be looking for. I can say this book will help you develop a hunger for the presence of God. I believe it will give you hope and the motivation to read the Bible and run after the desires of God's heart to become all that you have been created for. I believe we can live to the fullest of our potential. I believe we are powerful beings here on earth. I have been changed in such a radical way! My life became totally different. I became fearless. I have become so bold

I feel like I can take on the world, not in a prideful way, but in a commanding and demanding way spiritually. This is how God made us. I hope this book will help you to become stronger and pull you into a closer relationship with Jesus. I hope it helps you to go more in-depth with God and transforms you into a beautiful, amazing intercessor for others. With leading and guidance from the Holy Spirit, I hope this book will help you to become a deeper worshipper of God. I hope you pull things out of yourself that you never thought you had as you read this book. I also hope and pray that you are challenged so even your thought process is not the same. I hope you think deeper with God. I hope you ask more questions, and lastly, I hope you become closer to God than you have ever been. I believe you have already been radically changed!

God wants us to love Him every day. He wants to be there for us in everything we do, stay close to us, and direct our path in the right direction. "Trust in the LORD with all thine heart; and lean not unto thine own understanding. In all thy ways acknowledge him, and he shall direct thy paths" (Proverbs 3:5–6).

He wants to reason with us. He wants to be our closest friend. It doesn't matter who you are, doesn't matter what you have done, doesn't matter what your circumstances. He wants you to be close to Him. "Come now, let us reason together, saith the LORD: though your sins be as scarlet, they shall be white as snow; though they be like red crimson, they shall be as wool" (Isaiah 1:18).

Why? because He knows the plans for our lives. He knows what we can do. He knows how to direct that path in us. He wants us to come to Him, so He can reveal that we can depend on our relationship, faith, and desires in Him.

For I know the thoughts I think toward you, saith the LORD, thoughts
of peace, and not of evil, to give you an expected end. Then ye shall call
upon me, and ye shall go and pray unto me, and I will harken unto
you. And ye shall seek me, and find me, when ye search for me with all
your heart.

Jeremiah 29:11–13

The mind of God is a mystery, but His purposes for our lives are not hidden from us. He will make mysteries known to us. He wants us to know and understand His ways so that we will know and understand our purpose. We will also understand His will more deeply, which is the beauty of becoming yourself. We will find the answers we seek by knowing our identities, who we are, and our assignments from God. Becoming yourself means you discover Him in you. There is nothing in this world more beautiful than when you know what God your Father says and thinks about you. He says, Come, let me tell you a little about yourself. He will affirm your identity and everything you are, and you will come into this amazing relationship with your Father. This will change your life forever. You will be in your full purpose and potential and walk in fulfillment of who you truly are! When God speaks to you and affirms who you are, there is nothing like it! When this happens, nothing can change it, and you become totally and radically different.

The Way the Body Functions

There is a way that the human body functions, and while this is something most people know, some people do not know nor understand. Your body adapts to or becomes familiar with whatever you spend your time doing. So if you spend time watching TV, playing sports, playing games, or at the gym, your body takes on that nature and adapts. The more you do something, the easier it becomes because you are familiar with it. This is also true about our walk with God. The more time we spend with God, the more our bodies adapt to that pattern with Him, and so it becomes easier for us. The more we ask Him questions, talk with, and associate ourselves with Him, the more familiar we become. Everything becomes easier as time goes by. We are more familiar with Him, so it becomes easier to function. The more we understand His voice, the more we learn His ways.

Over time, our body becomes familiar with things we are unaware of, so whatever we do becomes easier. This is something you can judge for yourself. I'm sure you've done things that became easy after you put in the work. Finally, it became like a walk in the park for you. Since we develop all these abilities and have trained ourselves to become accustomed to habits without even thinking about them, they become natural and easy. You might not be good at basketball or football, but it becomes easy for you to do. You might not be a number one draft pick, but the game becomes easy for you to do because you spend time playing the game.

What if we take the same ideas and turn them toward God? We can develop an amazing relationship with God! How beautiful would it be if it became easy for us to spend time with God and ask him questions about ourselves that will change us forever? What if we train our bodies to grow naturally into the ways of God? What if we go to Him so often, and everything He does amazes us? What if we develop this amazing love relationship with our Maker? What if this closeness allows God to share thoughts that will endow us with amazing desires and a deep passion for reaching our fullest potential? I use potential often because I believe if we exceed what we are called to do, we fulfill the great purpose we were created for.

My Obsession with the Holy Spirit

I spent so much time with the Holy Spirit but wasn't even aware of what was happening to me. I was obsessed with the Bible, God, and His presence. I am even more obsessed with Him today. He is still my number one and always will be. I could not read, and the Holy Spirit taught me how to read by reading the Bible every day. Today I cannot count how many books I have read. I have gone to school and completed assignments my professors have kept because they had never seen anything like them before. I have my greatest teacher, the Holy Spirit. The more I read, the easier it became. At age 20–21, for the first time in my life, I was reading and saying words that were more than two and three letters. It felt so good and amazing that I wanted to do it every day!

The beauty of it all is that most of the time, it felt like the Holy Spirit was in the room. Wherever I was reading, I would stop and talk with Him. There's nothing more beautiful and precious than knowing the presence of the living God is with you and you get to have an amazing time talking and sharing with Him. It never grows old! It is fresh every day. Spending time with the Holy Spirit is a beauty I live for daily! Being in His presence has taken me places that I could never imagine. I cannot explain Him enough. The more I spend these times with the Holy Spirit, the more sensitive I become with Him, which is why I give everything to Him. My life is not mine. It's His because He makes me what I am today, and I will never forget that. I could not speak. I did not understand words, so I did not know how to use them, yet by talking to the Holy Spirit, He taught me. That's amazing, right? It gets even better! Spending quality time in the Bible did something to me that changed my life forever. The Holy Spirit started talking to me in ways I never knew existed, and

I became bold! I now do things I could only see in my dreams and mind that I never knew could become a reality. Since meeting the Holy Spirit, I have read more books than I can count, shared with thousands on huge stages, and on Jamaica's biggest religious TV show. I have traveled to many nations, shared the gospel, met with government officials and prime ministers of nations, and the list continues.

What We Carry in Us

All of my accomplishments became possible by Jesus through the work of the Holy Spirit in accordance with my Father God's will for my life. He taught me everything I know: to read, write, speak in public, and have confidence in myself. When we know the will of God for our lives and what His heart desires when He speaks, it changes us forever. Everything about us carries the weight and wealth of the kingdom of God. Everything about God makes a difference in us, so we walk in fulfillment in who we truly are in God our maker. We carry the wealth of heaven and the culture of the kingdom of God in us. We reflect the invisible God and make Him known and visible in a world that needs hope. We bring solutions and answers to a culture that needs God.

This is the culture of the kingdom of heaven. This is the place from where we shape the world. My brothers and sisters, this is what happens when we know the will of God. It is as if we open God's mind and come face to face with His thoughts for us. Knowledge and understanding of God make our faith so much stronger. This is my favorite part. Ready? We allow the kingdom of God to become the kingdom of man. In other words, whatever the Holy Spirit asks, that is what we do. We look and sound like Him until His desires are fully completed. Everywhere we go, we leave marks of His kingdom. Lives are affected by His presence in such a way that they become His kingdom. We are the ambassadors of heaven sent by God to be shaped and bring the culture of the kingdom to earth. We allow the things of God to become the things of man. That will happen in our homes, communities, schools, workplaces, and nations when we take on the culture of heaven.

All of this is revealed by God. This is what a relationship with the Holy Spirit does. It brings us closer to God and creates a bond between God and us. He shares His heart, mind, and thoughts with us. He opens to us in ways we never imagined He would, and that's what the presence of the Holy Spirit does. He brings us closer to God, our Father, and reveals the truth about who we truly are. When God speaks to us about all the things that concern us, it makes all the difference in the world. We are charged and changed; our minds renew; our hearts connect to His. When we understand what the Holy Spirit is speaking over us, we change radically and become unstoppable. In this closeness, the Holy Spirit reveals the deepest things about the Father's heart concerning us.. Knowing and understanding His mind and heart will always change our mentality, worldview, and mindset to bring us into a new place with God forever and ever.

WE ARE A KINGDOM FROM ANOTHER PLACE

We are a kingdom from another place. This is something most Christians, or most people, struggle with. It's a huge part of our identity. As a writer, I do not aim to confuse or leave anyone with any misunderstanding. I am passionate about my identity, which is first identified in Christ. I am formed from the dust of the ground, just a body created by God for a particular purpose and one uncommon reason. The purpose of God's spirit is to live in a body created from the earth. It is the most important part of his creation: humanity. It's not just the body but the spirit given to us by God, the spirit that lives in us humans as a holy temple for His dwelling and service, the communication and relationship with Himself. We are not of this broken world or designed to live in it, but because of sin we were turned out into a world that was not prepared for us, shut away from our true home. But we see in Revelation 21 that this true home will one day be restored to us. I hope my readers understand when I say we are from another kingdom and a different place.

Why is it so important to know who we are? Or why is it even necessary for us to come in contact with such reality? This is a question every one of us must answer for ourselves based on our relationship with Christ or time spent with the Holy Spirit learning about our assignment here on earth. To understand the weight and the value of His purpose in us, we must go to the place with the One to whom we are identified. Our identity marked us with whom we truly are and from where we come. It's not a mystery and should not be confusing. It should leave us in a state of uncertainty. If we have identified with Christ, if we are called by Christ, if we suffer with Christ, and if we die and are buried with

Christ, we will also be risen with Christ. "Now if we be dead with Christ, we believe that we shall also live with him. (Romans 6:8). He said it in this way,

Even when we were dead in sins, hath quickened us together with Christ, (by grace ye are saved;) And hath raised us up together, and made us sit together in heavenly places in Christ Jesus.

Ephesians 2:5–6

That is my true home: the presence of the living God. God created my body from this earth to carry His most valuable and pure possession, the spirit which was breathed in us and we lived.

God intended the garden of Eden to be the home of man from the beginning because it is the atmosphere of worship and the place where the presence of the Lord is. We were designed in that place with purpose. That is why men and women are without a sense of purpose or an atmosphere of worship today because they have lost the value of who they are. When man was turned out from the presence of the living God, from the atmosphere of worship and hope and fulfillment, into a world that was not ours, he lost the value of purpose. Mankind lost the value of their true self and did not find their in God anymore. Man loses his identity whenever he is taken out of the presence of God. I am thankful that one day, with all hope, that will be restored, as it says in Revelation 21 and 22. Man will live in the fullness of His identity before God in that atmosphere of worship in the home prepared for us from the very beginning.

For us to have a full impact on the earth, I truly believe that we must come face-to-face with and answer these questions:

Who am I?

Where am I from?

What is my purpose?

The answer to each of these questions comes from a relationship with God. To know who we are, to understand and walk in our purpose here on earth, and to fulfill the Father's will, we must honor what God has called us to. The Father's intention from the beginning of the creation of man was to be in relationship with us and allow His kingdom to come on earth.

So what are we going to do about it? How will we impact this generation and bring the culture of heaven into this world we are passing through, with all the gifts placed in us? It's to bring God's glory on earth. We must exceed the ability to do all that we are equipped with. We have always been kingdom citizens from the beginning. We are in Christ from the beginning, so we were destined to do great works just like Christ. That's who we are. Wouldn't it be beautiful if we colonized earth with the culture of heaven? That would be amazing and would bring the Father joy.

It Carries Value

Nations and nationalities are very important in today's culture. Believe it or not, it is what identifies us wherever we go. It doesn't matter who we are, our status on earth, whether we are wealthy or poor, kings or presidents, queens or ambassadors, we have to identify with where we are from, and it has to match our identification.

So where we are from identifies us, right? So, what about what we do? What about who we represent? What about our assignments? What about what we are gifted with? I hope this will have you thinking, and I believe it is going to change something in your life now. God told Jeremiah in Jeremiah 1:5, "Before I formed thee in the belly I knew thee; and before thou camest forth out of the womb I sanctified thee, and I ordained thee a prophet unto the nations."

I tell my kids I am their second father, their earthly father. Their actual Father is the true and living God, their Maker. I am just the one God used as a gateway to bring them into this world. Their true identity is first identified with God. I am a physical feature of what they are on the outside. The truth is what is on the inside, the very image and likeness of the Father, His spirit which gives us life. This spirit, which allows us to function, comes not from this world but from a heavenly kingdom. When I die, this body goes back to the earth. That is the truth. But the spirit that lives in me goes back to the Father, to its home and dwelling place. The body has no more value, but the spirit always carries its values. "Then shall the dust return to the earth as it was: and the spirit shall return unto God who gave it" (Ecclesiastes 12:7).

Which of these do you think has the greater value? What was created for the spirit which will go back to the earth from whence it came, or the spirit itself, which goes to live in glory with the Father?

I believe I was blessed and given an assignment I am equipped to carry out: to accomplish and fulfill His plans and purpose for me while I am living in this world. So at the end of my life, my loving Father will say, "well done, good and faithful servant" (Matthew 25:23).

God created all of us with power, authority, and dominion to accomplish and fulfill our purpose. Our nature is driven by that every day. Part of us will always be uncomfortable when we are not walking in fulfillment of that, so this has become our biggest battle or struggle.

This is my biggest question to you, and it's not a judgment nor a condemnation. I just feel the need to ask my readers this question. Who can you answer to? Are you the one that walks in fulfillment of his true potential? Or are you the one who is just going through life?

One of the greatest things in life is when a man knows what he carries and what he's worth.

This is the reason I am so in love with the Holy Spirit. He is the driving force, energy, and engine in us. What He can do with us if we let Him is unbelievable, which is why a relationship is so important to God. A relationship with God is where we find trust, stability, hope, a sense of purpose, and freedom to function in our calling. It is so much easier for the Holy Spirit to powerfully and effectively work through us when we have this amazing relationship with God. It gets crazier. Some say heaven is on earth, some say it all started with the big bang theory, some say life just happened, some say they have no idea, and for some, it gets crazier still. I believe this is the reason a relationship with God is so important. He can share His heart with us when we are in a place to understand Him and spend quality time with Him. I believe He loves to be with us. We must love to be with Him also.

The Holy Spirit Comes to Speak the Truth

And I will pray the Father, and he shall give you another Comforter, that he may abide with you forever; even the Spirit of truth; whom the world cannot receive, because it seeth him not, neither knoweth him: but ye know him; for he dwelleth with you, and shall be in you.

John 14:16–17

I have opened my heart to the Holy Spirit, and he has never disappointed me. He has never left me. He is my greatest inspiration, teacher, and my most valuable possession on earth. I depend on the Holy Spirit for everything. I call him my legend. He's my best friend and the only guaranteed truth I trust.

I do not want my amazing testimony to be complicated, but I believe it is important because our bodies were created from the dust of the earth, and our spirit is from God. So when we die, our bodies return to the earth and our spirits return to God, Himself. This is very deep, and I would love for you to go a little further in your devotional time for more clarity and understanding. The Holy Spirit will guide you. I can guarantee that you will leave with wonders about who God is in your life and think differently about who you are.

I am a person who loves to go back to the original, the very first and most important. Genesis tells the beginning and the life of Jesus models what is best for me. I believe we are from a pure and holy place. Our first house, our body, was created as a pure and holy place. It was in the garden of Eden where God created the first body and called it man, or Adam. He created his body for a greater purpose, to house the spirit of life, which gives man life. God gives directions and a sense of purpose through this spirit in us. I believe there is communication between the spirit in us and the spirit of God and that we learn the ways of God through this spirit the body carries. I believe that's amazing.

I ask my son this question often. Who are you, and what is your purpose? We went through Genesis together, the beginning, and he saw he was created for a purpose on earth. He knows he can make a difference in someone's life. So, when I ask him who he is, he tells me who he is: he knows he is a son, and he is on this earth for a purpose. My heart is that we would become bolder and stronger as believers to walk in the power of our purpose and God-given ability to become and do more. We have a great calling in our lives. Look at what happened in the book of Acts 2. God wants to do that with us because He wants to do what He said He would do in the book of Joel. It is not a mystery that He wants to do this in this generation today. He is doing it already all over the world. He wants us to become all He has destined us to be. Whatever you feel God is calling you to, that thing you find yourself doing every day, that you are passionate about, and that no matter what you do, does not leave your mind or heart, do it with the power of the Holy Spirit. He will bring that desire to pass in you, meeting you where you are on the earth for the kingdom of God.

We Are Attached to Him

God loves us so much that even though He is God, He wants us to love Him back. Let me share something important with you, so please don't go crazy. This book is more about the relationship with God and God expressing Himself and revealing Himself to me in a remarkable way, some of which I don't even know how to express. It is very personal to me after so many encounters with God that have completely changed my life. It has ripped me apart and kept me in His presence for more than twenty years. I am still hungry and thirsty, still crazy for the things of God as if I'm falling in love with Him all over again. His love is amazing, and I'll tell you something beautiful, He owns my heart.

Do you ever think about how special and unique you are or how loved you are by the Father? It is so amazing that out of everything God created, we are the most unique of them all. We were created, shaped, and formed by God in His image and likeness.

And God said, Let us make man in our image, after our likeness: and let them have dominion over the fish of the sea, and over the fowl of the air, and over the cattle, and over all the earth, and over every creeping thing that creepeth upon the earth. So God created man in his own image, in the image of God created he him; male and female created he them.

Genesis 1:26–27

Here we go again with more questions. Questions only you can answer for yourself. This is what makes these questions amazing. The answers can come from a relationship with God, our Father.

Why did God make us in His image and likeness?

Why did he name us Himself but bring everything else to man to name?

Why did He then give man dominion over them all?

What does his image look like in us? When I look at all the nations, tribes, and tongues of the earth, I see and understand how diverse God is in the creation. What is that one thing that changes everything? Even our vessel of clay contains something way beyond what we can see on the outside. I believe it is the spirit of the living God dwelling in us. It is not the skin, culture, or the family we were born into that identify us with our Maker, but our spirit that walks in the ways of the Father and models the fruit of the Spirit. The spirit within us demonstrates the image and likeness of God, displaying His nature and character in and through us. That is how this image looks. This is what I believe about the way of heaven and how the spirit of God works in us.

But as many as received him, to them gave He gave power to become the sons of God, even to them that believe on his name: Which were born, not of blood, nor of the will of the flesh, nor of the will of man, but of God.

John 1:12–13

In John 3:5, "Jesus answered, 'Verily, verily, I say unto thee, Except a man be born of water and of the Spirit, he cannot enter into the kingdom of God.'" I believe if we get this into the core of our spirit we will never be the same again. There will never again be a day of going to work, a church service, and doing life. I pray the Holy Spirit would be so connected with us and show us who we are in Him, to take us to the next level, a greater dimension in our spiritual walk with Him, and make us the bride prepared to be received by Christ.

We Belong to Him

When God made man from the dust of the earth, man was an unoccupied house. Man could not move or speak and had no sense of purpose. He was just the image of man. Then God did something that would change the molded clay forever. God released a part of Himself into that molded clay when He breathed into man's nostrils the breath of life, and man became a living being. "And the LORD God formed man of the dust of the ground, and breathed into his nostrils the breath of life; and man became a living soul" (Genesis 2:7).

This is why we belong to Him. For this reason, He pursues us so much, which is why this world will never be our home. There is a place where we will live in His presence. That is why Jesus came back for us. We are His from the beginning. That is why Jesus has to retrain, and teach us the ways of the kingdom all over again. We came from the greatest royal lineage and we belong to Him. God will never let us go or give up on us.

Let not your heart be troubled: ye believe in God, believe also in me. In my Father's house are many mansions: if it were not so, I would have told you. I go to prepare a place for you. And if I go and prepare a place for you, I will come again, and receive you unto myself; that where I am, there ye may be also.

John 14:1–3

I was lost and broken. I had no sense of hope or purpose. I was living day to day, and I had no value in life. I did not know who I was or any meaning in life, but my Father restored it all to me. I should not be alive today, but God did not allow that to happen because He had bigger plans for me that I am walking in today. I am so happy to be called His. I am very proud to be God's son because He has spiritually restored me to His original intent for my life. That is what He wants to do with every living human being on the face of the earth. If we open our hearts to Him and submit to His leadership, He will restore us all. He has a great desire for us. "The LORD is not slack concerning his promise, as some men count slackness; but is longsuffering to us-ward, not willing that any should perish, but that all should come to repentance" (2 Peter 3:9).

God did not create us to live outside of His presence or an atmosphere of worship where we can be with Him daily. I belong to Him, and He is the reason I am alive today. I know we all belong to Him. I also believe that no matter what we do, He loves us just the same. He will honor those who honor Him and punish those who dishonor Him. I want my life to be a life of honor and worth everything He made it to be.

Living in this world outside of the presence of God has nothing to offer me but brokenness, hurt, and pain. Man was created to be in the garden of Eden, in an atmosphere of worship, and in the presence of the living and holy God. We were not made for a life of disobedience and sin where we hide from the presence of God. "And they heard the voice of the LORD God walking in the garden in the cool of the day: and Adam and his wife hid themselves from the presence of the LORD God amongst the trees of the garden" (Genesis 3:8).

This is the beautiful and perfect will of God since the beginning. His intent is for man to live in this atmosphere of worship forever because it is a pure and holy place. The garden was a beautiful and joyful place where God and man enjoyed an amazing love relationship every day. Then this happened,

> *And when the woman saw that the tree was good for food, and that it was pleasant to the eyes, and a tree to be desired to make one wise, she took of the fruit thereof, and did eat, and gave also unto her husband with her; and he did eat. And the eyes of them both were opened, and they knew that they were naked; and they sewed fig leaves together, and made themselves aprons. And they heard the voice of the LORD God walking in the garden in the cool of the day: and Adam and his wife hid themselves from the presence of the LORD God amongst the trees of the garden.*

> Genesis 3:6–8

Because of this, man was driven out of the presence of God.

Man's disobedience broke God's heart, and since that day, man has been running from the presence of a living God, from his very purpose, and consequently has lost his identity and the value of who they are.

His Love: The True Heart of the Father

This has wrecked me as I am writing this book. I would love you to look back and think through this with me. Imagine God looking at man in an unfamiliar place, seeing him now broken and lost. But a loving Father will do whatever it takes to get his children back home. That's exactly what God did. He created a way for us through Jesus Christ and the Holy Spirit. Some respond to Him by receiving Jesus, and some reject Him by not receiving Jesus, which hurts the Father. I remember the first time I said yes to following Jesus. I gave my heart to Jesus that magical night. I felt something amazing and different that I had never felt before.

God wants to show us so much love. He has been doing it in smany ways, yet many of us have missed it. He wants to come to us in simple ways so we can understand and share His love. He wants us to love him back in unbelievable ways. This love comes from His presence and walking in obedience with Him. It comes from having a constant relationship with Him, hearing His voice and running in that direction. It comes from walking in honor of His will and instructions. It comes from making Him our priority. It comes from Him being preeminent in our lives and it goes on and on and on. This is the place God wants us to be with Him, to do what He wants us to do. He wants to restore us to Himself again.

Revelation 21

Anyone humbled by the leading of the Holy Spirit to walk before the Lord and honors Him as the Savior will find redemption in Jesus Christ. When that great and glorious day comes, we will be restored to our home, Eden, the place where the presence of the living God dwells. That is where I was created to be forever and where I will worship God. I will sin no more, and there will be no corruption. We will eat from the tree of life and live. I will glorify God in the trueness of a pure body created as a temple for the Holy Spirit.

What? know ye not that your body is the temple of the Holy Ghost which is in you, which ye have of God, and ye are not your own? For ye are bought with a price: therefore glorify God in your body, and in your spirit, which are God's.

1 Corinthians 6:19–20

I don't know about anyone else, but I want to be in the presence of such an amazing, loving God who has shown me so much love and mercy. I want to be in the place the Father intended when He created us, and I cannot wait for that glorious day to come.

WHAT CAUSES YOU TO DREAM?

The glory and presence of the living God have never left the earth. What God did many years ago, he never stopped doing. The relationship he shared with Enoch in Genesis 5:24, "And Enoch walked with God: and he was not; for God took him," was an expression of the relationship God wants to have with us. Intimacy keeps us close to the heartbeat of the Father. Melchizedek, the priest of God mentioned in Genesis 14:18–19 "And Melchizedek king of Salem brought forth bread and wine: and he was the priest of the most high God. And he blessed him, and said, Blessed be Abram of the most high God, possessor of heaven and earth" is a beautiful example of the remarkable way the many hidden treasures on the earth are connected to God. Even if nobody knows it, God will always find a way to make those treasures known.

Genesis 5:24 and 14:18–19 depict a brief entrance and exit of these two beauties. These are just simple men, but they choose to live a life of honor before the presence of God, and God made them known throughout history and the world as lives we can reflect on as we humbly walk before our Father. I truly believe He is looking for simple men and women to this today.

He found simple men who became great. In Acts 2, we see the disciples of Jesus receive Holy Spirit, poured out upon them, and they changed the history and the face of Christianity by making Jesus their center.

They also carried out the great commandment in Matthew 28, a life they had never dreamed of. They became men recorded in history. I believe you and I will become history makers and changers in this generation. I believe God wants us to dream and desire His ways so He can teach us His life pattern and display His glory on the earth, using in unbelievable ways.

There is a beautiful and glorious place awaiting us,

In my Father's house are many mansions: if it were not so, I would have told you. I go to prepare a place for you. And if I go and prepare a place for you, I will come again, and receive you unto myself; that where I am, there ye may be also.

John 14:2–3

That will be the most glorious and amazing day ever. There will be no greater joy than to be with Christ forever finally. I believe, however, that before that precious day comes, God wants to do something supernatural in and through us on earth. He wants to pour out His Holy Spirit upon His sons and daughters in ways we have never experienced before, as it is written in Joel 2:28, "And it shall come to pass afterward, that I will pour out my spirit upon all flesh; and your sons and your daughters shall prophesy, your old men shall dream dreams, your young men shall see vision."

God wants to use us, you and me, simple men and women, to cause an impact for the kingdom of God through Jesus with the leading of the Holy Spirit. God wants to open our capacity to His visions and dreams through the power of the Holy Spirit. We are all visionaries and dreamers. Everyone has hope for the future. We all have hope for what we want to become.

There is absolutely nothing wrong with us wanting to dream and dream big. What we dream of that determines whether that dream will become a reality. We dream of success, but what kind of success? Is our success only to benefit ourselves? Is there a place in our dreams for Jesus? Is our bigger vision for what we dream of reflecting Christ's kingdom?

I still have dreams of things I hope to do someday. But something has taken priority over all of my dreams for my natural, physical purposes. God showed me something that changes everything, and that's okay. In fact, it is great because I am walking in a greater purpose in the dreams God has placed on my heart.

There are two types of visionaries and dreamers. People have dreamed many things in many different ways, but they all fall under two types. There are physical dreamers and spiritual dreamers. I have never seen anything in between. It is one or the other.

This is very important to understand that dreams and visions influence where you go in life. They affect your function and purpose. Dreams also carry out your potential for greatness, which always comes with an assignment, something an individual must do in this life. This assignment is key to who and what we serve as we see visions and dream in this world.

The physical dreamer seeks to honor the things and purposes of this world in his achievements. On the other hand, the spiritual dreamer seeks to honor God's purpose for their life by putting the things of the kingdoms first. Which one are you? The one who honors the achievements of this world or the one who walks in honor of Jesus? These are questions you and I can only answer for ourselves. The Word says in Proverbs 18:16 (NKJV), "a man's gift make room for him." I want my life and what I carry to be a part of what God is doing on earth.

I felt different when I got saved and asked Jesus into my heart, but nothing supernatural happened. I was just a regular churchgoer. There were times when there was a move of the Holy Spirit. This would happen to different people in the church and there was evidence that something special was happening. It was not a performance, . You could tell this was something different and real.

As these beautiful movements of the Holy Spirit happened, I felt nothing, But as I thought about these movements, I started dreaming of this happening to me. Words were spoken, "the Spirit of God is in this place," and even though I felt nothing, I was amazed. I believe this is where my greatest desires and dreams began. I wanted the things of God I saw before my eyes.

I want to see men and women from every nation, tribe, and tongue set on fire with a hunger and a passion for the presence of the living God that will shake this earth like never before. My first encounters with the Holy Spirit changed the way I live and walk before God unto this very day.

Three events happened that I want you to be aware of. Two of those events were on the very same day. Here we go.

The First

The youth department at my church has an annual camp meeting and hikes the to Blue Mountain Peak, where Jamaica grows its famous coffee beans. The church was having a revival meeting.

A friend told me about the youth camp in such a way that I knew I could not let the opportunity pass. He had been there before and spoke with such passion and joy. He said it is like you are in heaven. You will feel God's presence and He will set you on fire. Then he said something that became my turning point. He looked at me and said, "if you come you will be filled with the Holy Spirit" because that is where he was baptized with the Holy Spirit. When I heard him say that, he did not have to say another word. I was hungry for more and wanted to be baptized with the Holy Spirit. So that was my ticket to youth camp.

I thought that what I read in the book of Acts about the Holy Spirit would happen to me. I dreamed of that moment and I could not wait to get there. I was very excited because all the youths at church were talking about going to camp, and I had never been to any camp in my life. Though I did not know exactly what to expect, I knew I would meet with the Holy Spirit. I have always loved the Holy Spirit and desire more of Him.

The presence of God was so rich and thick from the moment we arrived at camp. It was something more powerful than I had ever seen. That weekend was filled with young people being filled with the Holy Spirit, speaking in tongues, crying, worshipping, kneeling, and lying on the ground before the great and glorious God. That weekend wrecked me. I was touched and filled with the Holy Spirit and felt God in ways I can neither explain nor express.

The Hunger for More

Things that happened to me that weekend, more than twenty years ago, haven't stopped. I developed a burning hunger for the presence of God. That hunger and desire have never gone away. I tell you the truth: I am more in love with God today than ever.

After that camp, I started having amazing dreams. I would lay in my bed but couldn't sleep, butterflies in my tummy. I had crazy and amazing thoughts concerning the things of God. I wanted to be in His presence forever. My prayer time began to change, and I spent crazy time with God. Our love relationship is wild. I started taking on meaning. I start to see myself, my purpose, and my value in ways I had never seen in myself or thought of before. I had a messed up life growing up; I couldn't read or write. This was so different for me. Something was burning in me, and I started to see my value and purpose. The more it burns, the more I feel like I cannot stop. If I leave this world today, I can say I have lived a life before God, and man, was it was worth it.

I love the church I was raised in. When I got married, I began attending my wife's church. But my church and its youth group loved me and always encouraged me even though sometimes I felt embarrassed. For more than twenty years, my life has been a testimony to God in so many different places.

God wants to fill the earth with His glory. He is looking for souls filled with passion for Him. God wants us to find purpose in the things of His kingdom so that He can give us visions and dreams that will come to pass. We are all purpose-driven and filled with the fullness of God. We have so many resources and heaven stands in agreement with us:

> *And I say also unto thee, That thou art Peter, and upon this rock I will build my church; and the gates of hell shall not prevail against it, and I will give unto thee the keys of the kingdom of heaven: and whatsoever thou shalt bind on earth shall be bound in heaven: and whatsoever thou shalt loose on earth shall be loosed in heaven.*

> Matthew 16:18–19

The Holy Spirit was all over my life. He became my main focus. He wants men and women who are completely His.

> *Know ye that the LORD he is God: it is he that hath made us, and not we ourselves; we are his people, and the sheep of his pasture.*

> Psalm 100:3

> *But now, O LORD, thou art our father; we are the clay, and thou our potter; and we all are the work of thy hand.*

> Isaiah 64:8

The Second Decision

The second of these three events was very hard. The first one was easy. It was weeks before the other two. I was still in that burning honeymoon phase with God, and the youth group was planning a camping trip. I really wanted to go, but the church was having a revival, and I did not want to miss it either. It was hard wanting to be with the youth but also wanting more from God. Dreams can point you in the right direction, which what happened to me.

Before this revival service, I told myself, "if I experienced God at the youth camp, this is going to be greater." God did something amazing in me again. If God gets you where He wants you, He will do what He wills for you. Hands were laid on me as a young believer, people prayed over me, and words were prophesied over my life. I have walked in those words. I am living in some of these words today.

I did not go with the youth group. Although it was a dream of mine to return to Blue Mountain Peak, I also dreamed of the greater pleasure of being with the Holy Spirit. That surpasses my dreams for my personal desires, and honors the dreams that will help me exceed and become who God wants me to be today. I pray that your dreams and your desires are the same and that you are in love with the nature of who God is.

With all that is happening in the world today, God needs our availability so that He can take us to the place where He wants us to be. We should not base our dreams and desires on things of this world but keep them rooted and grounded in the things God desires for us.

You may ask, what does this have to do with having dreams? Or how do dreams relate to who I am in God? Dreams help shape our future and make us who we are meant to be. A person needs to have dreams because our purpose lies in them.

We desire many things, and many of those things come to fruition as we dream. The beauty of dreaming about the things of God is that can bring us into His presence, willingly and openly, so God has our full attention to shape us into what He wants us to be.

God wants to be our only God and our main focus. Only a handful of Christians are completely sold out and committed to Jesus. This breaks my heart, and I want you to imagine how God feels. I am not judging nor condemning anyone. This is just the truth. I also believe many are dedicated and sold out to Christ. This is also true.

The Holy Spirit is our greatest inspiration. He wants to inspire us with the beauty of God. The Holy Spirit wants to fill us up with the wealth of heaven. The Father wants us to dream desires for Him. He wants to pour visions and dreams iton us. This brings us to our purpose here on earth. He designed us and longs for us to long for Him. He wants us to be passionate about Him, filled with His joy, set on fire for His kingdom, and led by Jesus with the fullness of the Holy Spirit.

As you read, I pray and declare that you will not be complacent, procrastinate, or lay back, but rise to the fullness of who the living God made you to be. I speak into your giftings and purpose so you will be all God called you to be.

Where are the spiritual dreamers in the kingdom of God, Daniels, Abrahams, and Ezekiels? Where are the Deborahs, Naomis, and Ruths? Where are the Esthers, as "such a time as this" comes to fullness?

The fact that I am alive is a miracle. I should not be alive today. There is no way I should be sitting writing this book. No way. I fell in love with the Holy Spirit, and He began to teach me. There is no way I should be among a group of youths who saw a man running to the hospital with his finger cut completely off. We put his finger back on, prayed over him, and his finger moved. We sent him on his way, healed. No way, my friends.

Walk in favor with God, and He will find honor in what you do for Him. Be someone God uses to do something significant on earth in your lifetime.

WILL I PAY THE PRICE?

Jesus said to the Father in Luke 22:42–43, "'Father, if thou be willing, remove this cup from me: nevertheless not my will, but thine, be done.' And there appeared an angel unto him from heaven, strengthening him."

His purpose was for you and I to be reconciled to the Father. For that to happen the greatest price of all time would have to be paid through Jesus, for a lost people and a lost world. Just thinking about it brings tears to my eyes as I write. This is why Jesus is my greatest role model.

I try my best to pattern my life after His. As I read about Him I try to put His teachings into practice, not for practice's sake, but to actually live them day to day. He often prayed early in the morning, but He was in a constant relationship with his Father throughout the day.

I have grown to love praying in the morning. To model the life of Jesus, I get up early in the morning, away from any distraction, and pray. He made Himself available to anyone for the kingdom of God and shared the gospel to many. I am not going to say I have been the greatest example of walking the life of Jesus, perfectly doing exactly what He did. But my life is based on what Jesus did and said about how we should follow Him.

One thing I know with certainty is that our life should be a reflection of Jesus, so the world may see Jesus through us. Many will be healed by Jesus through us. Many will find salvation in Jesus through us. We are called to carry the image of the gospel to a dying world. We should bear the image of the cross so the world may see the price Jesus paid for our redemption.

Jesus bears the true reflection and image of the Father in ways that honor and represent Him. It is precious and amazing to me when Jesus says, He does only what He sees the Father do, in John 5:19,

"Then answered Jesus and said unto them, 'Verily, verily, I say unto you, The Son can do nothing of himself, but what he seeth the Father do: for what things soever he doeth, these also doeth the Son likewise.'"

While it is a very high price to pay, there is nothing more beautiful than to honor Christ in the same way He honors His Father. I believe this is what we are called to do. This is the life reflection, we should live. We should do nothing without Him and we should be guided by Him to do the things He taught us in His Word. When we are driven by purpose we take on meaning in life. This is what the life of Christ looks like. I pray you will see it, because this is how we are changed and transformed. Everything we do is done through Jesus.

Yes, the life of Jesus and the way He lived is a marvel to me as I read His word and spend time with Him. This is the same relationship I hunger for. This is what I live for every day, to be with Jesus, to know Him more, to spend time in the presence of the Holy Spirit, my best friend. When I am crazy in love with the things of Jesus, I ask the Holy Spirit to show me and make me understand the ways of Jesus more. He teaches me and I go crazy for Jesus. Because He honors the Father, He walks in full dominion, authority, and power on earth.

I must say though, it is not easy in this day and age to be completely committed and sold out to following Jesus. The way He pursued His Father is how we should pursure Christ. It's not easy, but this is a commitment I made early in my Christian walk. Anything for Him is worth paying the highest price. As you read on you will see I gave up something huge because He told me to and He takes first priority over my life.

We are all called to follow Jesus every step of the way. It is the only life for the body of Christ. Jesus is only way. As great as the men and women of the Bible are, we were not instructed to follow or be like them, but rather to be like Christ. That's the greatest price to pay.

It Must All Be Laid Down

We have to die to our own desires and agenda daily. If we are going to pay this price, it has to take something that costs us everything. It has to be His agenda, not ours. Jesus said,

> *Then said Jesus unto his disciples, If any man will come after me, let him deny himself, and take up his cross, and follow me. For whosoever will save his life shall lose it: and whosoever will lose his life for my sake shall find it. For what is a man profited, if he shall gain the whole world, and lose his own soul? or what shall a man give in exchange for his soul?*

Matthew 16:24–26

The world will also hate you,

> *If the world hate you, ye know that it hated me before it hated you. 19. If ye were of the world, the world would love his own: but because ye are not of the world, but I have chosen you out of the world, therefore the world hateth you.*

John 15:18–19

I could give a hundred reasons why the Lord wants me to write this book, and all of them would be important and inspiring. However, my agenda is not only to write inspiring stories but to share about the Holy Spirit and how important He is to the body of Christ. He is the easiest person to fall in love with, yet that's the hardest thing for a Christian to do. It's the hardest thing to get our attention. The Holy Spirit is the anointing and the power of the Godhead and the greatest gift to us today in the body of Christ. Yet we pay Him the least attention.

Relationship Matters

Here we go. Thfor you to have a relationship with Christ through the Holy Spirit. The Holy Spirit is the wellspring of life to all who come in contact with Jesus. Jesus did this daily, showing us how to live every day in a relationship with the Father. He did everything right all the way to the cross. He fulfilled His purpose of bringing redemption and a relationship with the Father to humanity.

Many Christians don't know who they are or what their purpose or calling is in the body of Christ. This is where the Holy Spirit comes in. This is why He was given to us, to bring to pass all of the things Jesus spoke about, open our eyes to the things of Christ, and empower us to walk in authority, purpose, and our giftings to fulfillment with power and dominion on earth. To do this, we must pay a great price and sacrifice. The question is: do you want this?

The Holy Spirit wants to do for us what He did in Acts for the disciples. But he can't find us. Why? Because we are too busy with everything in this world: sports, TV shows, social media, work, and much more. We give the least attention to the presence of the Holy Spirit. To many He may as well not exist. We can be good and genuine Christians who go to church and love the Lord, and that's great. But we cannot stop at just going to church and loving. The Lord desires so much more from us.

I Must Know

Let us stop going to church to listen to the sermon and then go home to the world of our activities. Let us start seeking Him, His desires, agenda, intentions, and will for our lives. Let us start taking Him everywhere and spending quality time with Him so we can take those encounters with Him to church. Let us see miracles, breakthrough healings, and signs and wonders in our churches. Let us be with Him so He can do what He wants to do through us and with us.

The Holy Spirit wants to show us our giftings. He wants to show us things that will blow our minds and take us to a whole new place with Him. Do we want to be there and know? When we know all these things, our relationship with Him makes a big difference. More than sixty percent of Christians don't know their purpose or what they are called to do. Those Christians may spend only five to ten percent of their day with God, including church. Those who know who they are spend fifty to eighty percent of their time with God. That is a difference.

My main purpose is that many will fall in love with the Holy Spirit. That is my heart for this book. He will show you all that you need to know. Ask Him to be a part of your day and your life. Talk with Him throughout your day, even at work, and you will be amazed by how He responds.

The Price for Our Desire

I have faced many turning points and encounters in my life, some more costly than others. This was one such encounter.

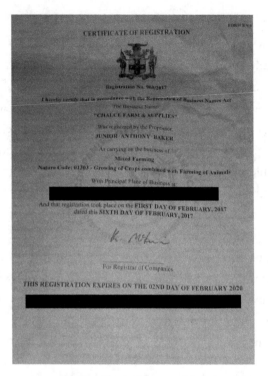

This is my company brand certificate and license. This was going to be it for my family and me. It was going to change our lives and finances forever. I was getting ready to sign two big contracts that would make a few million Jamaican dollars. I was in the United States just having a simple conversation with the Holy Spirit. We have always had this love affair. No matter where we are, we have quality time together.

The Lord said something to me, "Close your business down. I want you to do something for me." I had already made a few hundred thousand from the business, and things looked good. It wasn't an easy decision, but I was willing to pay the price for what the Lord wanted me to do. So I closed the business. I called my wife to tell her what the Lord had said to me. I had her handle all of the paperwork to close the business down. It was a very hard decision to make, but I did.

His price was way higher than my desire. It's never about the money, but always Him. I have made a commitment to God that I would pay the highest price for anything He wants me to do.

He called me to go to the nations, and that's what I'll be doing for the rest of my life. His desires come first, not mine, not for money or anything else in this world. Only what He wants for me. Trust me. I have spent the last twenty-plus years doing just that.

A man's purpose is key in his relationship with the Holy Spirit because the Holy Spirit is what makes us unstoppable. This is how we are shaped. This is how we learn the voice of God. This is how we learn obedience and truth, and it's also how to grow in character.

I know I speak of the Holy Spirit a lot. He is the reason my life has changed and transformed because He allows me to. He is the reason for this book. If I take Him out of it, it would be worth nothing but good for the trash. It would have no value or purpose. I would rather write a book with the Holy Spirit all over it than write stories that sound beautiful but have no effect.

I wish we would talk about Him more every day and spend more time with Him, sing more songs about Him, and preach more messages about Him. The greatest life we could ever live is talking about Him and being with Him. That's how we learn and carry His wealth as He transforms us.

The Holy Spirit and Jesus, Son of the living God, are my best friends. I talk about them and anyone who knows me knows most of my conversations are about them. I fell in love with a God who makes my life worth living; I don't ever want that to change. I will make my whole life about Him, and that's all that matters to me. I do everything to the best of my ability for Him.

WE MUST START BIG BECAUSE GOD STARTS BIG

God is the God of great power, wealth, authority, and prosperity. God is beyond bigger than how we see Him and view Him. We are limited as we look deep into the mysteries of God. Therefore, it is a challenge for us to understand Him. We will never be able to say, "This is the beginning of God or this is as far as God can go." The Bible outlines where He started in creation, but not concerning His existence because it simply cannot. Yet we have scriptures that describe Him in unbelievable ways.

Bless the LORD, O my soul. O LORD my God, thou art very great; thou art clothed with honour and majesty. Who coverest thyself with light as with a garment: who stretchest out the heavens like a curtain: Who layeth the beams of his chambers in the waters: who maketh the clouds his chariot: who walketh upon the wings of the wind.

Psalms 104:1–3

This is the unbelievable part. This is where I love to fellowship with God. This is also God's most valuable place with man. This is where God shares deep things with man. As you read in the introduction to this book, the foundation of this book is me, the author. God's most valuable possession is His relationship with man. This is where He reveals His heart's intentions to man concerning what He wants to do and how we play our part with Him. This is key to who we are, becoming what He created us to be, fulfilling our purpose, walking in our destiny and calling, and using our gifts and talents.

I want you to understand one very important thing in this chapter. When God told me to write this chapter, He said, "Start big because I started big." This does not mean He wants us to go crazy without a clue of what we are doing. He wants us to know the greatest place to start is with Him. Only in Him are we big beyond measure, beyond our greatest expectation, beyond the limitations of this world. He wants us to know that He will put in us His very will and vision in the direction He needs us to go.

Where We Are Now

Where we are now with God is very important. I believe that even in the world today, God wants the body of Christ to open its capacity to see Him more than we ever have before. This cannot be just how we view church within a program or the environment of most churches today. We must become radical in our thinking, removing blinders from our eyes so we can see what God wants us to see. I believe God will do things that will blow our minds out of this world. He is calling the body of Christ to come closer to Him than ever before.

God is already showing many believers great things, and that could include you. We see these things but tell ourselves we cannot do them. Wake up, my friends. If God shows you something, He carries the wealth of resources to accomplish it. He is faithful to see His assignments through to the very end. Start big. See your visions as He shows them to you, and let Him do wonders through you now.

If we take ourselves out of the picture and allow God to be the center, He will do great things in and through us. He spoke a word to Abraham, and it made a difference. He spoke the word great nation, and Abraham moved concerning this great nation.

Now the LORD had said unto Abram, Get thee out of thy country, and from thy kindred, and from thy father's house, unto a land that I will shew thee: And I will make of thee a great nation, and I will bless thee, and make thy name great; and thou shalt be a blessing.

Genesis 12:1–2

The prophetic call was to Samuel in 1 Samuel 3.

He approached Saul on the road to Damascus and commanded him to reach the gentiles with the very gospel of Jesus Christ he was totally against. This transformed his life forever.

And as he journeyed, he came near Damascus: and suddenly there shined round about him a light from heaven: And he fell to the earth, and heard a voice saying unto him, Saul, Saul, why persecutest thou me? And he said, Who art thou, LORD? And the LORD said, I am Jesus whom thou persecutest: it is hard for thee to kick against the pricks. And he trembling and astonished said, LORD, what wilt thou have me to do? And the LORD said unto him, Arise, and go into the city, and it shall be told thee what thou must do.

Acts 9:3–6

God wants us to see what He wants to do with us, and He wants us to start there. Like these and many more men in the Bible, and even more not written about. Even in our day and age, God wants to do something significant with us, and the greatest place for us to start is in His presence. Yes, we will see things others say are impossible, but we know all things are possible with God. Let us start to do significant things and become significant today. Let us see God in such ways that history will remember what God did in our lives. Let us start something that will leave a legacy and inheritance to our children and grandchildren.

Are We Comfortable/Satisfied?

Sometimes many of us, including myself, have lost our relationship with the presence of God. It's not because God stops speaking to us or removes Himself from us, and it's not even because we are not seeing or hearing His voice. Instead, it is because so many other things occupy us.

Sometimes we get caught in uncertainty because there is a struggle between what we see and hear from God and what society demands from us. It becomes a battle or struggle, and we become uncomfortable with where we are with God.

Our relationship with God and where we are going is so important. We should never settle for less when we know there is so much more. We are not satisfied when we feel and sense that our spiritual nature is screaming out for more, wanting to be in that place where growth and development take place.

The key to who we are and getting where we need to be is this simple answer: a relationship with God. That relationship with God will drive everything great in us. I have talked a lot about the Holy Spirit, Jesus, and being in His presence; Why? I believe we are created to be in that atmosphere of His presence. I believe that place is where we see, do, and become.

This is a place where many Christians struggle. I have been there before and struggled until I saw something the Lord did. I became hungry, passionate, and driven to spend time with the Holy Spirit. That has rooted my faith in Jesus, brought me face-to-face with the Holy Spirit, and changed my life forever. I know I've probably said that a million times in this book, but becoming yourself, walking in the purpose of man, and shaping kingdom-culture is worth His time and being in His presence.

I know there are many great books out there about purpose. Many give directions on how to get there and will help you. That's great, but for me, there is just one thing that separates a person from this world: the Holy Spirit. He will teach us all we need to know and become. That's where I point everyone who reads this book. The Holy Spirit will shape what matters: y our character and purpose.

Transitioning

God is a multicultural God. He does things in many different ways. He does miracles in many different ways and speaks to different poeple in different ways. That's just Him. Our lives, personalities, and callings will always differ because we are all unique, special, and specific to God.

Transitions mean a lot, and there are different ways of transitioning. But we have to know what God says and when He says it. We have seen Moses go through many transitions: first pharaoh's daughter's house, second out of Egypt, third back to Egypt.

And Moses said, "I will now turn aside, and see this great sight, why the bush is not burnt." And when the LORD saw that he turned aside to see, God called unto him out of the midst of the bush, and said, "Moses, Moses." And he said, "Here am I."

Exodus 3:3–4

This is where it's at. If God can get our attention so that we turn to see Him, focus, and come close to hear Him, then the sky is the limit, and greatness will be our reward. If God can get us to see Him and hear His instructions like Moses at the burning bush, my, my, my.

When the conversation at the burning bush was over, Moses had a heart-to-heart connection with what God wanted to do. He saw everything clearly and understood. What he saw was bigger than himself. But He who gave the instructions was able and was bigger than the instruction itself.

He saw and heard, and that's all God wants from us: our attention. Our purpose and assignment are of most value, and there is nothing else we need to do but trust Him. He will do the rest. That is all He desires from His people: their attention. He seeks the availability and attention of the body of Christ and that is the hardest thing for God to get. He does not have problems with the work. He has problems with finding those to do the work.

The greatest place anyone can start anything in life is from where they can see the vision. We see men and women making a significant mark in the history of this world throughout the Bible. They could do it because they saw something greater than themselves that God wanted to do, and they responded.

All He needs from us is to say yes to Him. He will do the rest. I said yes, and He made me into someone amazing and beautiful. I saw it, and it became the big picture in my head. I pursue Him, and He brings plans to completion. I'm still working on it. I have been blessed to be in places where some of the greatest movies are filmed. I've been among the richest in first class, flying back from a nation with my family. I've been on TV shows, stood on stage with a multi-Grammy award winner, and stood where governments have stood, seeing many lives change and come to Jesus. I've seen and experienced miracles. I came from one of the roughest communities and knew nothing, and now I have been with the wealthiest of the wealthy.

This was all possible because I started big. I saw the big picture of what God wanted to do with my life, and I allowed Him to work my character to see it come to pass. I believe there is so much left God will do throughout the nations of the earth through me. I believe He will change lives throughout the nations with my life because I have seen it, and I have already started. I have left a mark on nations.

I will never see or think small ever in my life again. God does not have small visions and dreams. God does not do anything small. Everything He does points to salvation in Jesus, whether healing, miracles, salvation, or revival. All of it is to the glory of Jesus so we can redeem what was stolen from us: a relationship with the Father. Nothing about that is small. He's more than enough and bigger than we could ever think, imagine, or dream. We can do it. We can think and live big because it's not us. It is all in Him, the Son, and the Holy Spirit.

THE GOD IN YOU

Before creation, before the beauty and splendor of heaven, before all glory had been revealed and seen by angels, before the wonders, works, and beauty of creation existed, before all harmony and great power, uniqueness and majesty have been seen and expressed, He was and will be forever.

And the four beasts had each of them six wings about him; and they were full of eyes within: and they rest not day and night, saying, Holy, holy, holy, LORD God Almighty, which was, and is, and is to come.

Revelation 4:8

The beauty of God is that He fell in love with the world, atmosphere, and environment that He created. "Thou art worthy, O LORD, to receive glory and honour and power: for thou hast created all things, and for thy pleasure they are and were created" (Revelation 4:11).

Who wouldn't love a God like this? How can we not fall in love with Him? Why can't we see Him in all the beauty around us? How could this beauty be missed and misunderstood in so many ways? This God lives in us and gives us the uniqueness of His presence; we breathe Him night and day. That blows me away! The Creator loves me. What a joy to know that His greatest creation is man.

The beauty of this amazing and loving God is not only that He exists but all He has created and brought forth. Creation is His most beautiful and priceless possession. Proverbs 8:23–31 expresses a beautiful, intimate, and close-up relationship in such sequence. It poetically expresses the works of God. Speaking in amazing ways about this adorable God and His creation is wise. It is breathtaking to be in tune with such a God. He is so amazing. But it is Proverbs 8:30–31 that blows me away, "Then I was by him, as one brought up with him: and I was daily his delight, rejoicing always before him; Rejoicing in the habitable part of his earth; and my delights were with the sons of men."

This beautiful master designer who lives in us wants to take us places in Him we have never been before. He wants to decorate us with the wonders of heaven and shower us in the fragrance of His love. This beautiful God wants us to know He is still in love with us and wants to be in tune with us. He still wants us to move in rhythm and sequence with what He wants to do on earth.

What Can We Do? Nothing, Just Love Him

He is unmovable, unstoppable, and unchanging. There is nothing we can do to stop Him from loving us because we breathe Him, the spirit of the living God. There's nothing we can do to make Him deny us. We bleed Him. The blood of His son Jesus Christ runs through us. We are in harmony with the Creator. I cried many, many, many times thinking about what I have done. How could I deserve such love? How could I deserve such a God? But it is not about who I am, but who He is.

A man's encounter with Him begins when a child comes forth from the womb. God is the first thing they see when they open their eyes and the light is there. He is the light of the world. The first thing they do is breathe God, the life given to the first man. The Spirit of God is why this beautiful Creator is a masterpiece and a joy to be with.

I deeply love my wife, and we have an amazing love affair we have shared for more than twenty years. I have amazing children I love dearly, and there is nothing more important to me in this world than my family. Yet the love and relationship I share with God are way above what I have for my family. Nothing will ever come close to or take this love relationship away. Nothing is worth more, or can pay the price for it. It cannot be bought. The God in me cannot be replaced. There will never be a substitute for the God I fell in love with. I will never exchange the God who took me from nothing and did wonders for me.

The God who is writing this book will always be my wonder. He will always be my greatest desire. He will always be my most precious treasure. He will always be the one who inspires me. He will always be my greatest vision and dream. He will always be my most refined gold, priceless rubies, and precious pearls. He will always be my most outstanding one. He is the one I live and die for. I will always be amazed by His beauty and wonder. His presence will be my greatest comfort and most treasured place. He will always be the splendor of my heart and the one who stole my heart and allowed my eyes to gaze on Him. I will always desire His secret place. For Him, I will always rejoice. The God in me is my greatest wonder. How beautiful is this amazing treasure and wonder to me: my God.

The Truth

I look around and see the wonders of this amazing God. I realize that it is not in a building or system. No matter how precious we make something, it is not there. It is not in any special or specific place. It's in us! "Now when Solomon had made an end of praying, the fire came down from heaven, and consumed the burnt offering and the sacrifices; and the glory of the LORD filled the house" (2 Chronicles 7:1).

He did not come because of the temple, though it was prepared to embrace His presence. He came because Solomon asked Him to come. The greatest place He wants to be and dwell in is us, not a building. He doesn't need sacrifice. He needs our hearts. He doesn't need a burnt offering. He needs our obedience and faithfulness to Him. The greatest place we can prepare for His presence is in us. That's what God values the most. That's what led Jesus to the cross.

Our purpose and desires are not for us. They are for Him. We are equipped to fulfill His will, which is why He is working from within us to carry out His greatness in us. All that we are points to this one specific thing, to redeem what was lost in the garden through Jesus Christ. Our gifts, talents, what we are called to be on the earth, miracles, signs, wonders, and the outpouring of the Holy Spirit all have to do with one thing. "And I will put enmity between thee and the woman, and between thy seed and her seed; it shall bruise thy head, and thou shalt bruise his heel" (Genesis 3:15).

How could I not love a God like this? The One who fulfilled His promises and is faithful and true to His commitment. The beauty of who He is and who He created us to be is the alignment of our purpose: to be with Him forever. This will occur when we submit to His lordship, walk faithfully before Him, and let Him do all He wants to do in and through us. We must make ourselves available to Him. He would never let the enemy win because He loves us that much. I see His reflection all around me on earth every day and the way He uses men and women to bring forth His glory for the greater cause of the kingdom.

And when he had taken the book, the four beasts and four and twenty elders fell down before the Lamb, having every one of them harps, and golden vials full of odours, which are the prayers of saints. And they sung a new song, saying, Thou art worthy to take the book, and to open

*the seals thereof: for thou wast slain, and hast redeemed us to God by
thy blood out of every kindred, and tongue, and people, and nation;*

Revelation 5:8–9

I will never regret the day I said yes to Jesus and entered this beautiful relationship with God. In all these years of walking with God, I've learned things so many I had never known and have been through so much. I came to understand there is one place I was created to be: with Him. Nothing satisfies me the way His presence does. Nothing gives me peace and comfort the way His presence does. I can bring Him no greater joy than what I am doing now. I love Him as I have never loved Him before.

All that I have come to be, my purpose, abilities, and gifting, the spiritual wealth God has given me, the way He shapes my life, and the many who came to know Him have nothing to do with me, but everything to do with the power and glory of God. He loves us beyond measure and wants to show Himself through us day after day and night after night so that all His children will come to know Him, receive Him, and walk in His love.

Nothing is about me. None of my accomplishments are about me. They are all for His glory and for the promises He makes. They are all for His purposes in us. I responded to Him, and He took a life of trash and made it beautiful for His kingdom. I will always owe my life to Him and be His servant. I will always serve Him to the fullest and best of my ability. I will go all the way for the sake of the gospel through Jesus Christ and the work of the Holy Spirit through my life. I will die to this world and live for the glory of His kingdom.